Dear Claudia
Thank y
for taking ...
to read this book
❤ Deborah

Her Secret Sins

Her Journey From Prostitute To Princess

DEBORAH SCHREPPER

ISBN: 978-1-5356-1012-4

Dedication

Writing this book has been a reflective journey.
At times, it was difficult to talk about the intimate
details of the lowest parts of my life. I would like to
dedicate this book to every woman who ever found
herself in the same conditions, and to the survivors,
the overcomers, who fought their way out of the
darkness and haven't looked back. You can make it
and you will make it! And this book is also dedicated
to my father, who is my "superman." He never gave
up on his daughter and loved me through it all. It
is also dedicated to the memory of my biological
mother, Judy, for without you I would not be here to
tell my story, and your tender message to me on your
deathbed has changed me forever. But most of all,
I dedicate this book to my mother, Julia, who loved
me without condition and never looked back. She
never questioned her decision to love me, raise me,
and teach me how to be the woman I have become. I
love you more than you know, Mother. Thank you for
choosing me so long ago.

Table of Contents

Introduction

My journey, my path, has been a rocky road with hill after hill to climb. It has been said that when you're climbing a mountain, it gets harder toward the summit. Indeed, it does, but every time I would fall down that hill something inside me told me to get up and start climbing again. My worn and tattered shoes have walked me into disgusting lows in my life, but like journey of the lotus flower, beauty and strength was growing within while I was within the mud. This is my testimony, and as you can guess, it includes a few tests.

Chapter One

We often say the cliché "You can't choose your family." But in my case, my mother's longing to have a child of her own and the sadness surrounding the circumstance of why she couldn't carry one led her to me––therefore, she did indeed choose me. My mother chose me to be her daughter when I was five months old. I was born to a heroin addict, and then accidently broke my adoptive, my true mother's heart. Eventually, when I was twenty-six, I had the pleasure and honor of meeting my biological mother, and we developed a cordial, and eventually beautiful relationship over the next eighteen years until her death, in 2016. Then I was privileged, once again, to not only attend her funeral but also speak about the woman, Judy, who brought me into this world. A wonderful experience that I will never forget.

I stand at the end of my parents' dock on the lake I grew up on, looking out on the cove protected by trees.

To the left of our private beach is a peninsula with rocks leading up to it and trees that have survived difficult storms, leaving some broken in half. On any given day, you can find a few snapping turtles in the water, reminding you to beware its deceitful beauty if you choose to swim out to the peninsula. I look around at the seemingly peaceful, albeit lonely, scenery. I close my eyes, take a deep breath, and hold it as I take a leap of faith and jump into the murky, unclear waters beneath me, leaving the safety of that solid ground I was standing on for the past nineteen years…

Chapter Two

I was eleven and in fifth grade, and I was relieved when my parents said we were moving to Winthrop, to that house my dad had fallen in love with on the lake.

On one of our Sunday-afternoon drives, about forty-five minutes away from our Davis Avenue house, my dad had taken my mother and me along this beautiful road that had more potholes and faded tar on the streets than us city people were used to. As I endured the "I Spy" games I frequently played with my mother on road trips, my dad was pointing out how peaceful this town was and how he was now familiar with its surroundings because his successful company was close to the town. This tired and, by now, bored young girl perked up as we passed a small beach that even had a dock to walk out on, and I saw the children jumping from that dock into the lake! I looked as we drove past some beautiful homes along the lake that were seemingly nestled in between the tall trees. The yards and shrubs were so eloquently manicured that I suspected this was where all the rich people with well-behaved children lived. Rounding the corner on Memorial Drive, about half a mile from the beach, my dad saw it! He slowly moved past this brown house with white trim and a lawn that wrapped around another, smaller house, a guesthouse. Looking past the guesthouse, I saw a giant Christmas tree (or at least what looked like a giant Christmas tree). My dad turned around and pulled into the driveway.

"Dad, where are we? Do you know the people that live here?"

My dad, the stereotypical New Yorker that he is, turned to my mother and me and said, "We are going to live in this house one day. Just you watch."

Laughing out loud, I thought to myself, *my dad is crazy!* My father was the ultimate negotiator; I believe he could talk a goldfish out of his fishbowl if fish could comprehend.

The owner of that house was a short Jewish man and his wife with big, bulging eyes. She looked different than people I knew in my city neighborhood. And they had a daughter, Mary, but she was probably as old as my parents so at that time I didn't understand why Mary was an adult child living in her parents' house. *Doesn't she have a husband or kids? Or even a dog or cat? She's awkwrd*, I thought to myself.

I came to know these people over the next few years, and I can understand now why she lived there. She was quiet, but odd. She had very poor social skills; however, she was extremely smart and appeared to be very tidy, but in an OCD-type way. As a teenager, seeing this woman, I felt bad for her, never seeing anyone her own age nor any love interest. Her books were her best friends, and due to the contents of those books she most likely knew a lot about everything.

Well, her father was not interested in selling his home at that time, but my father gave him his card and told him, "Sir, when you are ready to sell your house, call me and I will give you what you ask for it." Predictably, one year later we were living in that house on the lake for a mere steal. Not only did my dad buy the house, but the man sold it to my dad with everything that was in it! I think the gentleman didn't realize the goldmine he was sitting on, because even in the uneven garage's attic there were some truly priceless pieces and photographs that told the story of this house and its birth. To this day, I'll never forget the pictures, the guesthouse, or their odd and yet special daughter.

They all moved to Florida after that and we would visit them a few years later on one of our Disney World trips. Sarasota was, after all, where all the people with money would retire, eventually leaving their legacies behind with future generations. I don't know what ever became of Mary or all her books. She was past childbearing age then so I know she didn't have children. And I'm sure her parents are long deceased now, along with whatever dreams and hopes they had for Mary.

Chapter Three

I was told at one point in my life that there is a thin line between reality and paranoia. Up until that day, in Phoenix, Arizona, six months after that moment on my parents' dock, I would have told you that you were incorrect and that there was no possible way one could intertwine the two. However, if that thin line was made up of baking soda and cocaine, then that line had already been crossed.

I'd moved to Phoenix after deciding I had had enough of the small-town living where I was the only black individual in that town. I had been blessed with parents who not only adopted me but provided me with an amazing childhood as well, and who taught me the value of hard work and didn't just put things in my hand. I had to earn and learn to work for the material things they provided me with. But I had an innate desire for living on the edge that my parents could neither foresee nor halt. I couldn't explain it, and after I got into serious trouble at my job, my father and mother agreed it would be best if I started fresh in a place where nobody knew who I was.

I became a stranger in a very strange big city, complete with the anonymity and the new beginning that I had longed for. I chose a city three thousand miles away that, unbeknownst to me at the time, would provide the opposite of the amazing benefits my parents shared with me. I would soon become a victim of my own curiosity and the behaviors genetically ingrained in me and succumb to my worst fears.

Six months after moving to this very large, overpopulated city, I finally met a friend, Lily Davis. She was really the only friend I had at that time, and she not only was my best friend and the girlfriend of my boyfriend's friend, but also became my dealer and, eventually, my lover.

After an exhausting evening of partying, I still didn't want to return to my dismal, lonely apartment, even though it was early in the morning, so Lily invited me back to her apartment. She had a seemingly quiet pad on the first floor close to the parking lot. It was bigger than my apartment and had a spacious living room with tall windows looking out on the front door. Her furniture was strategically arranged away from those windows so that anyone who entered was clearly visible without being blocked by her contemporary leather furniture and crystal-clear glass table. I wondered how someone could afford such nice furniture at our age. Lily appeared quite popular around town to this small-town girl. She always had company over that never would stay long, not even long enough for her to offer them a glass of water, which I wondered about and quickly came to understand why.

Lily came out of her dark bedroom (at least I assumed it was dark; I wasn't allowed in the back room) with a box in her hand and sat down next to me and said, "You can have however much you want." I didn't realize what I was truly looking at in the beginning and found myself gazing at what looked like the beautiful snow-covered mountains of Maine I'd skied on all my life. The powder was perfect and fluffy in its consistency, and I later learned it was in almost pure form.

Lily placed a small pile of "snow" in front of me and created this one-inch line. It reminded me of the aftermath of a snowstorm, when the plow trucks would leave a beautiful embankment of snow on either side of the street. I thought to myself, *why is she pulling a credit card and a dollar bill out?* She rolled up that dirty dollar bill and I watched her sniff that line through it like it was nothing.

After watching her, that innate addictive creature within me woke up and I knew I had to have one too, and so she made me my own line. I couldn't even begin to say how many of those little one-inch lines we did that night; all I know is that in an instant I was hooked and couldn't wait until I could see my friend again and indulge in this new experience. I felt so much power and strength and boldness after doing that line that when she embraced me, I didn't hesitate to return her advances and gave in to my wildest fantasy.

Many months passed, during which I was working at a wonderful makeup and skincare company––until I was fired because of my paranoia and attitude, leaving me jobless and unable to maintain my "fuel" each day. My friend, who became my lover on occasion, was gracious enough to provide me all the cocaine I desired in exchange for whatever she desired, whether it be cleaning her apartment or not. I was still barely maintaining my own apartment even after losing my job. I lived about fifteen blocks from Lily, which didn't help my love of cocaine. I was a slave to my addictions and quickly realized I would have to use my creativity to continue to pay for my tiny one-bedroom apartment down the street, not to mention to pay for gas for my shiny black Chevy Beretta. It was so easy to have this powerful white substance available to me that I often thought, *how can I make the green stuff available to me just as easily?* The innocence of that soft white powder called often and the answer became all too clear to me while blasting a line of coke up my nose, creating a burst of creativity: *my body.* My best skill was my body.

I was young, with light skin and long hair, and men always told me I was sexy. I drove down to the local strip club––you know, the "respectable one," where women only had to wear G-strings and be topless dancers. A few of the high-end bars would audition me, but stated, "Men don't want natural breasts, they want big ones." I took a blow to my self-esteem, but was not willing to give up on this newfound idea of stripping being a profession. The nude strip clubs were looking pretty tempting at this broke point in my life and so I thought, *Why not?* I had nothing to lose (so I thought) and I didn't look too bad.

The first time on stage I was a nervous wreck, but at the same time I liked the attention and, of course, all the money that flew up. I made sure to bring my "fuel" with me and had to do a line or two before my turn on that hard-black wooden stage.

After a few weeks at that club, I was coming back to my apartment one night and ran into my neighbor, Patty, who I knew was also a stripper, making more money than I was. What I didn't know was that she had access to information that I had never dreamed of. We went into her apartment, which was next door to mine on the basement level. She had beautiful things in her apartment, not eclectic pieces that never matched like the ones in my apartment. Her furniture matched her rugs, which matched the throw pillows on her sofa. She seemed very classy.

We sat down and she proceeded to tell me all about the Alaskan Pipeline, and that men would pay thousands when they came off their shifts of working on the pipeline at this little strip club that would fly girls from all over the world in exchange for an eight-week contract. The girls would stay there in the dorm up above the club. She stated that one of her friends had told her about this "traveling gig" and that we could meet with the woman who would interview us for the positions and have us sign contracts.

There was only one catch for me: you had to be twenty-one and I was still twenty for about another two weeks. But that was all I needed to hear; I already had a fake ID from my teen years. And after this woman interviewed us, she looked at my ID and said, "You're hired." She couldn't tell us much about the club except that it was in Fairbanks and that the housing was provided upstairs from the club. My neighbor and soon-to-be coworker––shall I say a fellow nude stripper––and I were on the next flight.

When we arrived in a small airport on a puddle-jumper plane, all I saw was a desolate land with barely any people and a lot of snow on the ground. It was freezing there and, coming from Arizona, I sure didn't have enough warm clothes with me in the one duffel bag I had, which just contained high heels and a few "costumes" I was able to purchase. I didn't know what to expect. Someone was waiting at the airport to take the fresh meat further back into the woods, to a seedy little dive bar that looked more like a cabin than a strip club. I noticed one restaurant a block away that looked like a local mom-and-pop place to buy food and get a hot meal.

When the driver said, "We're here," I was expecting some grandiose building with flashing lights, but no, it was just a cabin-looking bar. We were immediately taken into the front entrance, where a handsome white man in his late twenties sat on a stool; I assumed he was the bouncer. We handed him

our contracts and he asked us for our IDs. Patty had
hers and I had the fabulous fake New York ID that,
surely, these locals would never be able to tell was
fake. After staring at me and chuckling to himself he
said, "You don't think I would actually believe this
is a real ID, do you?" I was caught, ten days before
my twenty-first birthday. You see, you had to be at
least twenty-one to work in that club and since I
still had ten days to go, I wasn't legal yet. I thought
I was going to be sent back to Phoenix but, seeing
that I had already signed the eight-week contract
and that I probably could bring in lots of money to
his club, he generously offered what he considered
a deal. Now I see that he used a scare tactic: seeing
that I was thinking I would be arrested for breaking
a contract, he took advantage of my naïveté. Upset
that the woman back in Phoenix couldn't tell it was a
legitimate ID, this man said I could clean the club in
the mornings, vacuuming, wiping tables, cleaning the
bathrooms, etc., in exchange for ten dollars a day for
my food (which in 1992 wasn't bad).

At that same diner, I'd seen down the street,
for three dollars I could get a good breakfast, the
remaining money left I was able to get a few snacks
for throughout my day, and a sandwich for lunch. I
was usually starving by nighttime. If it wasn't for some

of the girls in the dorm offering me their Top Ramen soup, I'd really be starving. I would try hard to fall asleep on the three-inch mats that sat on the wooden bunk-bed-type beds. Most nights I listened by the door leading downstairs; I could hear music and a DJ. Sometimes girls would run upstairs for something, probably stashing money so they wouldn't have to tip the DJ and bartenders as much. And I would scurry off to my little lonely bed.

I lay there night after night, weeping. I was so hungry, so bored, so alone. I was isolated and unable to make money and couldn't wait until the following day for my ten measly dollars to go eat the biggest breakfast I could, knowing that I had no more money for the rest of the day. I don't recall how I was able to stretch that ten dollars to feed myself with enough food to have the energy to clean that nasty bar and stage.

Once when I was cleaning the pole and stage, I pretended I was already working and tried to spin on that pole, only to land flat on my backside. *Stupid sneakers*, I thought to myself, walking away laughing at the only thing that had brought a smile out of me in what seemed like forever.

A small, dark, skinny staircase toward the back of the club would lead you to the dormitory, which really resembled more of a minimum-security jail, or even a kennel where stray dogs were kept. My area–– you couldn't call it a room because the walls were only about five feet high and there were no doors––was a space no more than six feet by six feet in which there was a built-in bunk bed with a three-inch mattress on it and an open shelving unit with about four shelves to store all your belongings. And every stripper had a roommate. Down the hall there was a community bathroom. I can't recall the details of that bathroom; I just remember it was a big open shower with maybe four showerheads, like you would find at a summer camp, or a prison. My privileged upbringing had never prepared me for conditions like this. The girls were messy, leaving their clothes all over their cubicles. Even my own bunkmate was messy.

Some of the girls had shiny costumes and elaborate, expensive things. Those were the girls that had a side hustle. Talking to this short, chubby girl with big hips and a curvy bottom and long, straight hair, I asked her how much she had made so far. She didn't hesitate to tell me over twenty-five thousand.

"What!" I yelled.

She told me that all these men working the pipeline were almost sexually deprived, so most every girl working had those "side hustles": those men who just wanted sex, companionship, and whatever else they wanted, and weren't short on money. They would lavish on those girls' gifts, jewels, and, of course, money, which probably explained why I never saw the girls, even in the daytime hours. They were being pampered and performing other things to enhance their earnings while they were there.

After hearing stories from many of those women about their side hustles, I decided that was it! On the morning of my fourth day there, I decided this whole cleaning scene was not for me. I had just had enough; if I couldn't earn a thousand a night, like some of the others there had told me, I wanted to leave. *How* was the question.

During my few days of being there and, surprisingly, enjoying my talks and mealtimes with some of the women there, I'd come to be considered like their little sister. I wished I had known about the conditions before coming to the frozen tundra, but, never having been in this type of committed contract, I was a greenhorn. And at least I had a bed of sorts to lay my head on and a pillow to cry into.

I befriended one woman on my fifth day who was in the kennel next to mine. She was stunning at more than six feet tall with a slim build. Her skin was the color of a creamy piece of chocolate and her hair was in a short, loose Afro with beautiful dirty-blonde highlights in it. I didn't see Dawn when she worked in the club but I'm sure she wore some type of wig, since most men want to see a woman with hair longer than their own.

As we talked that morning, she informed me that she too was unhappy after being there four weeks, and wanted out of her contract. She was pretty much past the prime age as far as stripping goes, and she looked as though she'd aged out and was worn out, used up. She said she had a male friend in Seattle who was like her sugar daddy, and that he would send her money for a train ticket and she was sure he would buy me one too. Relief in my body came instantly. I thought, *this is how I can finally leave this place*, and, *how sweet is this man to buy a stranger an escape just because she's his lady's friend?*

I was so naïve, but nevertheless a plan was hatched, and the next day, while the other girls slept, we caught a cab from Fairbanks to the train station in town. It was a ten-hour ride to Anchorage. The old passenger train was basic in the interior and reminded me of a New York subway: no frills, no fancy, just comfortable cloth seats and, somewhere, a restroom. The ride was almost unbelievable as we rode through the untouched beauty of the Alaskan tundra. I saw only one small house or cabin along the way, and the rest of the scenic view was all snow-covered land. A part of me was expecting to see a few polar bears or igloos along the way, but when I didn't I just closed my eyes and imagined what my new friend and I would be into next.

We arrived in Anchorage. Dawn was kind to me; she knew I had absolutely no money and therefore she became my protector and a mother of sorts. She never told me how old she was, but by my estimate she was in her early to mid-forties. It became a recurring theme throughout my life that during dangerous times, when I needed it most, I always had a guardian angel around me.

It was bewildering to me that as many pockets of peace and tranquility and natural beauty there were in this land, there were equally as many dark and seedy places within the city. The beauty that was surreal had an opposite counterpoint in the many lonely and desperate men seeking service in this underground sex industry. There were so many strip clubs in Anchorage, and that made it easy to find work--well, for Dawn. I, on the other hand--well, I was forced to research escort services I found in the yellow pages and wound up at a brothel, "The Club." I had never been a woman of the night but certainly had the experience, and this was a job that I knew I could do.

From the outside of this club, you would never have guessed what exactly it was on the inside. It was just a house with a driveway; I can't seem to remember if it had a sign of sorts. However, when you walked into the front entrance you were immediately immersed in the elegance and old-school charm of how you would imagine a brothel looked in the 1800s. The doorbell would ring and all the women in the house would run to form a line, strategically placing themselves to be lucky enough to be noticed and chosen. You didn't want to be the first or last woman in that horizontal line; it was best to be second to the last or third from the first. Most of the girls working were all the same, seasoned professionals whose appearance resembled that of a porn star: blonde hair, large breasts that were all too apparently shaped with silicone as they stood at attention. They were barely dressed, leaving nothing to the imagination. A man didn't have anything left to see on these women.

How degrading to stand in a line near the door with other pretty young women, hoping some lonely man who felt horny whose wife wasn't giving him any at home would notice me and choose me out of this line of similar-looking girls was the thought running through my mind. I didn't understand the diversity I brought to the house and as the first man, whom I assumed was a regular, came through the door, his eyes landed directly on me, then on my breasts.

"Her, let me try her tonight," he said.

One of the veteran girls led me to a very swanky bedroom with a king-size bed on which were a deep-red silky bedspread and several pillows. There was also a beautiful bathroom with a jetted garden tub and separate shower. Later, I was told this was that gentleman's favorite room. While the veteran girl showed me the room, the man was taken into the bar area (*The guys get a complimentary drink and I get to put out my body,* I thought to myself). He was then led upstairs to the room. He watched me as I showered, a fetish of this man's; I supposed in his mind he preferred a clean whore and not a dirty one.

The feeling of being used to fulfill someone's fantasy was disgusting to me at first. I didn't like my body, so, why did they? In hindsight, I see that because I looked different I looked innocent. I was that greenhorn in this profession, so my words and actions weren't rehearsed, which in turn was a turn-on for these men, who were so used to the same thing every time.

On each nightstand were condoms in beautiful bowls. Real sexy, that was. Obviously, he said, "Darlin', let me see how you put this on. Do it real slow and look me in the eye so I can see your pretty eyes." If my lips were to voice the words in my mind he would've smacked me. *This pig! I have to lift your fat belly to even get to your tiny package and then you have the nerve to want me to look you in the eyes as I'm placing this thing on you? Why? So, when you go give your wife some, your mind can reflect back to the young sexy black chick you paid for that night! Just hurry up, fat pig!* I was thinking as he was moving up and down on me. Finally, when he was done, fifteen minutes later, I walked him downstairs to the "pay station," where he told the house manager how good I was, and he was so satisfied that he hugged me and whispered, "I left something for you on the nightstand, sugar." I had to return to the room afterward anyway to clean it up and sneak in another shower. Sure enough, he'd left me a tip, a hundred dollars, and I changed the sheets, as trained, so the next client could have a "clean" experience. I decided, *this is the easiest way to make money, I can do this.*

After that first client, my first call came in and they requested someone new and young, and a girl of color if they had one. So, my new employer sent me out with the driver/bodyguard. This was not a real bodyguard; he was a scrawny, long-hippy-haired guy who couldn't do damage to a mouse, let alone a big strong Alaskan man. The only thing that gave me a false sense of security was his .380 he carried in his holster on his right hip. At least he had a weapon; I only had a smooth and fast-talking mouth to get me out of situations.

The drive was more than thirty minutes and I felt as though we were in the middle of nowhere (which, in retrospect, we were). I walked up to the customer's door shaking and unprepared for what I'd find. Knowing this was an escort service, I'd known I would eventually be sent out on calls, but that couldn't prepare me for the reality of being thrown into a proverbial lion's den and not knowing what to expect, since every person's homes were not similar, like the girls and rooms of the Club. I knew at the Club I could push a panic button, aka intercom button, and someone would be up to the room instantly. This was only my second customer and I was hoping that I could live up to his expectations.

This salt-and-pepper-haired man in his forties opened the door and welcomed me in. I couldn't help but notice all the hunting paraphernalia, like the bear's head, deer antlers, and other wildlife on his walls. The only words I remembered him saying were, "You better be really quiet, my wife is in the basement asleep." After that I couldn't tell you what we talked about; I just wanted this hour to hurry up so I could get my money and get out of the creepy old man's house. Not only was I thinking I'd never see the outside world again, but I thought to myself, *Surely, he is going to make me his sex slave, and maybe his wife in the basement isn't really his wife but another prostitute he enslaved.*

After what felt like days instead of the hour that it was, I finished the job and he paid me the two-hundred-dollar fee and gave me a hundred-dollar tip. The tips were all mine except that out of my tip, I was expected to tip my driver, so I tipped him twenty. Back at the cat corral, as I called it, I turned in my fee, and out of the two hundred I walked away with less than a hundred. After that the rest of my calls were in-house. I made a few more hundreds and I quit. I might be a hooker but I wasn't stupid. I was the one working; why should I give my money to someone else?

Chapter Four

Dawn had been working at one of the strip clubs, though I still couldn't because of my age. We met up and both of us decided it was time for another adventure out of the deep woods of Alaska. And Dawn's same sugar daddy encouraged us to fly to Seattle, since this was the cheapest and closest to Alaska. Since I had money by this time, I was the one who paid for our plane tickets to Seattle, Washington.

Upon arriving in Seattle, Dawn and I were low on funds again, so that sugar daddy of hers flew in from wherever he lived to meet us and assist us in finding temporary work in Seattle. I was unaware at the time that his way of assisting us with work would mean having a few threesomes with my friend and me. He had rented a car and a nice hotel room and as I closed my eyes I tried hard to ignore the moaning sounds next to me. The next morning Dawn told me that he had given her a couple hundred for her "services"; of course, I didn't receive anything out of it except a plane ticket I'd already used and a nice place to sleep and a few decent meals.

We were only in the hotel for one day, and in the morning Dawn asked me to join her in going to British Columbia because we could make even more money working as legal prostitutes in some of the high-end cathouses there. By this time my twenty-first birthday had passed and I was of legal age to do anything I wanted. Excitement filled my mind as I thought of all the expensive things I could buy. I even imagined being the woman lucky enough to have the same encounter as the character in the movie *Pretty Woman*. That was a far stretch from the direction we had to take. Not even in the same class of women.

We left the hotel and walked the windy, chilly street down to the dingy, dark bus station. Waiting for our British Columbia adventure, we met these two tall, dark, somewhat handsome men. We talked with them for hours, exchanged numbers, and then boarded our bus, fully expecting that we would never see them again.

I had never been to this part of the Canadian border and was excited at the possibility of finally making that money that everyone talks about. I didn't realize that truly I was chasing something that I never would obtain. I was so sure at that moment that someone would pick me and recognize that I didn't belong in this industry. I knew in my heart some man would see the value behind my eyes and that my heart was pure as gold, and would make me his lifelong princess and eventually his queen. I was anticipating a shift in my dark life––which had been colored dark only because, I eventually realized, of the path I myself had created and chosen.

As we arrived in British Columbia and waited in the customs line Dawn informed me that a long time ago she'd done something that got her into serious trouble and that customs might not allow her to cross the border. She never would tell me exactly what had happened for her to never be allowed into Canada. "What!" I yelled. "You wait until we are already here at the border?" She thought that enough time had passed that maybe they'd just forgotten and would let her through. Well, you can imagine what happened: Dawn was denied access into Canada, and I didn't want to go alone. We had only purchased one-way tickets, and as we waited on the lonely wooded road going back into the USA the same bus that had taken us to Canada took mercy on us and offered to take us back to Seattle for free.

There we were, with no money, no sugar daddy, nowhere to go. We had given up and decided to sleep

in the Greyhound station. Dawn decided to call the
two men we had met in the bus station earlier that
day and see if there was anything they could do. It
turned out they lived very close to the station in a
subsidized apartment building. They came and picked
us up and let us stay there for a few days. One, Larry,
stood well over six feet tall with long shoulder-length
hair; he was surely mixed with black and Indian. For
someone I didn't even know, he was so respectful
and generous without expecting anything in return.
I learned a valuable lesson that day from this kind-
hearted person. Not every man, not every person who
helps you out in life, is seeking any kind of reward.
There are, sprinkled throughout the world, good and
genuine people who see the heart you possess. They
see there is good within you and in that recognition,
they are naturally compelled to help and guide you in
a better direction.

After what seemed like an eternity, Dawn left me
and went back to wherever she was from. She must've
been tired of this game as well, and was realizing
the adventure had gone as far as it could. She left
without saying goodbye; I never saw or heard from
this woman again. Larry was kind and mentioned I
could stay, but I was ready to go home. I'd just turned
twenty-one and already felt like a used-up old rag

someone decided to wipe their dirty floors with. No, it was time to swallow my pride. I gathered my belongings and went down to the payphone on the street and reluctantly called my mother, begging for her to Western Union me some money so I could get back to Phoenix. I thought to myself, *at last this nightmare is over and I can begin my life in Phoenix all over again.*

When I returned to Phoenix, I knew that I had to pay my rent and other bills, so I took yet another nude stripper job on the seedy side of town. This club was run by an owner that, oddly enough, owned most of the several strip clubs in Phoenix. It was named after an old children's television series, though there was no magic mirror with the lady saying, "I see little Debbie and Johnny and everyone else." This was one of the lowest times in my life, and this place was even seedier than the last place I'd been in.

One thing about me was that I never just quit or threw in the towel. I always made friends, even in the strip clubs. In this club, I met another woman almost twice my age. She convinced me to start that chase again for money, that dream that hadn't died when I left Alaska. I could still be someone's queen, there was still a chance, and she told me that we could make money in El Paso, Texas, where there were plenty of strip clubs and plenty of men willing to tip and pay for extra services. So, believe it or not, I set off on another adventure, driving my own car with this woman to Texas. I wanted to drive my own vehicle this time because then I had the control and the power to leave when I was ready. And Texas lasted about two days; there was no abundance of money. Only dirtier old men wanting a young girl to give in to their twisted fantasies. We returned to Phoenix with no more money than we'd left with.

I was still stripping at the local clubs in Phoenix when, sometime in July of 1992, at twenty-two years old, I found out I was going to be a mommy. I thought to myself, *this is the change that I needed, the start of a new beginning, a way out of the fast life and off drugs.* But you're only pregnant for nine months, and I was only clean and sober for about six months. The first three months of pregnancy, I couldn't help but to sneak a line of cocaine, and throughout my pregnancy I smoked my Newport Lights, never getting the willpower to quit smoking. At least I stopped doing cocaine for the next six months.

Lily and I never lost contact; she was thoughtful enough to have planned a surprise baby shower for me, and she was also expecting a baby boy. She had gotten married so I assumed she had created a better life for herself by having a complete family that was whole.

My parents weren't overly thrilled that I was going to be a single parent, but they embraced the fact that I was going to be a good parent. My mother and I were close but they didn't live in Arizona, so childbirth was left up to me, with my friends as my coaches in the delivery room. *Push!* was the word yelled at me continually. I would get tired, like the life I was trying so hard to bring into the world was at the same time leaving me too tired to keep up the momentum to keep going. Never one to handle physical pain, I was forced to feel the pain of childbirth without the drugs and without my mom being there with me in my delivery room. Oh, how I wished she could see me give birth. I knew she couldn't have a child naturally, so I had always wanted her to experience it in some form, and perhaps even to make her proud of me and of how hard I was working, without masking the pain, to bring forth this new beautiful life, her granddaughter. My new best friend, LaToya, was there with me, and as I pushed for the final time, ripping myself with a fourth-degree tear, I screamed and my daughter was now in the world.

Having a daughter was like having my own personal doll whom I could dress up and whose

hair I could put in ribbons and whom I could teach
all the wonderful things I knew. I asked LaToya if
she would do me the honor of becoming my child's
godmother. Her family took us in to teach me how
to even be a new mother. I hadn't grown up with
any experience with little kids, let alone babies. So,
LaToya and her family quickly became my surrogate
family. Her grandmother became my grandmother.
Before you knew it, my child was growing up
alongside all the other children that found their way
to that house on the corner, which was filled with so
much love nobody could walk away without feeling
loved and without knowing that Grandmother and
the entire family always had your back, and would
always look out for you and your children, despite
the condition you were in. To this day, they have
always shown me and my daughter and future
children unconditional love.

Being so proud of myself for not partaking
in drugs over the last several months, I
decided I deserved a little break. By this time
methamphetamine had hit the scene and I knew that
Lily, my old friend, would have the newest and best
form of it. I called her up. "Debbie!" she yelled with
excitement. We talked briefly on the phone and soon

our friendship had rekindled, and a more powerful drug accompanied it for the next several months.

One morning, after a difficult night spent at Lily's house, trying desperately to come down off my two-day meth high, the real paranoia had set in and all I could hear in my head was, "The Lord is my shepherd, I shall not want." I couldn't take this anymore; I hadn't slept and I was convinced I had completely lost my mind. Lily took me to the state mental hospital and promised she would look after my child for me. After what seemed like forever on the drive down to the 24th Street facility (and I was positive I had witnessed a few accidents, murders, and rapes along the way), we were there and I was in a safe place. The people did a brief intake and I signed a stack of papers, and then I had to say good-bye to my daughter. The intake staff took me past the lounge where patients could hang out and entertain themselves with checkers or writing in notebooks or coloring. I watched some of the patients as I walked by and thought I must be in the wrong place. I wasn't crazy; I'd just had a moment of paranoia after doing too much meth.

There was a woman by the window having a conversation with someone, but there was no one else there with her. Another man I saw was just sitting in a chair rocking by himself with a blank expression on his face. I would walk around in the confines of that psychiatric unit wondering why I was there. What was my purpose in placing myself there, in that condition? How had my life taken such a spiral to the bottom?

The doctors and nurses always spoke realistically to me, as I was most likely their only patient not there long-term. My psychosis was only temporary, brought on by the side effects of sleep deprivation and strong hallucinations from all the methamphetamines in my system. The nurses would joke and laugh with me. Some of the orderlies I watched intently, as they would often have to drag someone off because they were in a psychotic break. They would reassure me that I was just fine and not like the others at that place. Some of their words to this day resonate with me: "Young lady, you don't belong here. When you go home, you get your life together and don't put that poison in your body anymore."

There I was, in my room. There was only a small window with bars on the inside and a sink and a mirror. It was one of those plastic mirrors that distorted the way you look. I stood there for a moment looking at myself. My small five-foot-three frame was emaciated and my hair was dyed almost a mustard color. I no longer recognized the woman, the shell of a soul, that I saw in the mirror that day.

Lily's addiction was not as strong as mine. She could quit and not use without difficulty, but not me. I was genetically predisposed to be an addict. I'd used to think I looked fine, but the more I stared at myself the more I looked like a lost soul that had been sucked into drugs and that way of life. I looked tired, and I felt worn and used up, like a dirty rag that one refuses to throw away because they think, *I can get one more use out of it.* But eventually you realize it's no good for anything anymore and you throw it away.

I had only been doing meth for a few months. My daughter was only about five months when I started up and nine months when I found myself in the hospital. I only wanted my parents to be proud of their daughter. I didn't want them to regret choosing me as their child. I wanted them to refer to me the way they often did to my father's children. They, always in my mind, were successful. They had never brought shame to my dad; they were business owners and successful salespersons, with perfect marriages in which they raised smart children of their own. And then there was me, everything they were not: I was scarred, marked by a shameful profession, with no real desire or direction in my life, and now I'd managed to end up a drug-addicted, wasted, and washed-out prostitute. Not what any parent wants as a future for their child.

My mind was tired of planning, plotting, and hustling, and tired of the way my life seemed to endlessly drag me along for the ride. I was not living anymore; I was merely existing at this point. I wasn't even twenty-three years old yet and to look at me in that mirror was to see an old woman past her prime. All the while that same voice, the same sentence, came back in my head: "The Lord is my shepherd, I shall not want."

Unbeknownst to me, Lily had called my mother in Maine and she had flown out that next day. In between meeting with the psychiatrist and talking to the few sane people in my pod, I had slept almost all that weekend. I had gone in on a Friday and had come to my senses by Sunday. I was in my room trying to focus on reality when a staff member informed me I had a visitor. Trying my best to brush what was left of my hair, I straightened up and went to the visitor area.

Looking through the glass, I wondered, *what have I become?* I stood there mesmerized by what I was looking at. I was on one side of the glass, looking out at this beautiful, chubby little girl with a head full of the most perfect straight black hair. She was just nine months old and was already walking. Tears rolled down my face as I reached out to try to hold her and touch her. I wanted to pick her up, kiss her, and just watch her stumbling around as she perfected her walking technique. This beautiful child I was staring at through the glass was my daughter, my saving grace. She saved me with her unconditional love for her mommy. Full of vivacious life, full of joy, full of hope, and providing that boost of encouragement I needed in the exact moment I was ready to give up on myself, her tenacity for life wouldn't allow me to just give up; in fact, it did the exact opposite.

My mother had come all the way to Arizona, picked up her grandchild, and then come immediately to check on her daughter. I didn't think too much about what she had gone through at that time. But looking back on that experience many years later, I can only imagine the broken heart of my mother. Today I ponder the question in my mind: if she had known what I was going to do, to be, that I would put myself out there in such a degrading and demoralizing way, would she have still adopted me at the innocent age of five months old?

My mother hadn't hesitated or thought of the implications of adopting a black child back in the early seventies, a child that wasn't wanted because of her "mixed" color. She had always been my cheerleader, role model, and teacher. I'd always been a writer by nature and she encouraged that gift within me. She was a schoolteacher for many years, which hadn't stopped just because she retired. In 2014, I wrote a poem and presented it to her on Mother's Day when she came to church with me. As much thought as I put into the words of my poem to her, I put an equal amount of time and thought into the frame of the poem. To know that the only people who never gave up on me were the very ones I was letting down has brought me a lifelong desire for them to say it was worth the difficult years.

One Prepared

There was a woman who asked God for a child with many tears down her face

There was another woman who was with child and not wanting that child in her place.

So, God prepared both women and blessed them, but only one could be called Mother

One woman brought forth the child inside her, then her task was done

And the other woman gave the child love and real life like no other.

The child grew to know she was different and not
like the rest

She knew that two women were put to the test

One woman gave her the tanned skin she had

The other woman taught her to be thankful and to
always be glad.

One woman gave her a strong voice with which she
can sing

But the other woman gave her the tender heart and
the lyrics that she brings.

One woman brought this child into this world and
then her job was done

The other woman, with tears in her eyes

Well, her job had just begun.

The child standing before you today understands
there was no other

There could never have been a woman better
prepared

For the job of being my mother.

Twenty-three years ago, at the tender age of
nineteen,

I told my mother I wanted to move out of the great
state of Maine.

We packed a few things and boarded the plane,
3000 miles from home, seeking a positive change

I never could've imagined that my life would never
be the same.

My mother didn't know this land beneath her feet

Perhaps that's why we ended up driving the wrong
way on a one-way street.

Together we found a tiny dwelling space

She taught me and rode with me on the city bus
until I was able to find my way around this strange
place.

My mother returned to her state of Maine

And I was now all alone in a city that didn't even
know my name.

A few years later, I happened to meet a few peculiar
folk

And after much repentance

God blessed me and filled me with the Holy Ghost!

As I now pack up and leave this no longer strange
land

I just want to thank you and tell you I love you for
all these years when you held my hand!

Written by: Deborah Elizabeth Schrepper 5/11/14

With much reluctance, the psychiatrist, who was most
likely worried I would return to a world filled with
drugs or worse, decided that I was no longer a mental
misfit and that my paranoia and hallucinations were
indeed part of the methamphetamines that I had
taken, and he released me into the care of my mother.

My mother took me and my one-year-old
daughter back to Maine with her in the days following
my release from the psychiatric hospital. Maine was
so beautiful in June. The never-ending greenery
and the early morning calls of the loons on the lake
behind our house were enough to melt the heart of
any depressed and strung-out junkie. Our house
sat on over an acre of beautiful green grass with a

long sandy beach before the lake in our back yard.
There were two tall pine trees that sat to the right of
my parents' beloved porch that wrapped around the
entire back of the house, facing the lake. In between
these two aged and beautiful trees, my father had
a hammock hanging from them. This is where my
recovery began.

It probably took a good three days of what some
call "detoxing" my body before I began to feel a sense
of normalcy and could function again without the
assistance of crystal meth. I never went into a rehab
center, nor attended any formal programs; my old
friend the lake provided the much-needed peace,
and each day the loud noise screaming within my
mind began to diminish, and it became clearer and
stronger every day. I watched my daughter play on
the same beach that I'd once played on so many
years ago. The warmth of the sand between her feet
brought the sweetest smile to her face as she sat
playing with her shovels and pails while I meditated
in that hammock. It felt like God himself was rocking
me gently, letting me know that every crooked road
I'd crossed would become straight, and I would be
able to look back over my life one day and say that
despite it all I'd been blessed.

I stayed in Maine with my daughter and parents for three more weeks. Then my mother flew once again with us to Phoenix to help me re-establish my life there. When I did return, I started to feel as though there was something I was to do with my life. I took employment with a medical temporary agency shortly after returning to Phoenix, which allowed me to get an apartment with my daughter, a real home, where she had her own bedroom. It wasn't fancy and, truthfully, wasn't even in the best part of town. But we didn't care; it was ours and my daughter was excited to have her room to herself. I had some furniture from my old apartment and some of my surrogate friends/family in Phoenix to help us move. My mother had bought her a green metal twin bunk bed.

The apartment complex was a little bit run-down, but the husband-and-wife managers tried their best to keep it up. There was a pool and a patio with rusted metal sun chairs and a few tables. The first summer my daughter and I spent there, we lived out at the pool. She loved to swim and was very good at it. By the end of every summer, she was so dark from being outside all the time. The jobs that I held seemed to get better and better and eventually I landed a position at one of the elite hospitals in Scottsdale.

The mother of the man I'd been dating while I was pregnant with my daughter was a born-again woman, and she put her pastor on the phone after I returned from Maine. Now, I'd never told anyone the sentence that the voice had said in my head, convinced I was just high and becoming crazy. But my friend's pastor spoke to me on the phone that day and told me to find a Bible and read Psalms 23.

Never having opened a Bible, I didn't have a clue what he meant by a psalm, but when I opened the Bible I opened directly to that page, and there it was: that voice, that sentence, was not merely that of a lost crazy mind. Psalms 23 begins with, "The Lord is my shepherd, I shall not want..." I knew that voice belonged to God and that it was He who had rescued me.

I never touched cocaine or meth again, and I began going to her church. I'd never gone to church as a child so I hadn't had the opportunity to experience old-time religion. It was like no other church or feeling I had ever experienced in my life. This was an old-fashioned holiness church where people were not ashamed of praising God, and should you fall out of the pew or have snot running down your face, there was another sister or brother to catch you or wipe the tears and snot off your face.

The more I went to church, the more my heart began to open, and a feeling of conviction started coming over me every time I walked through those doors. I would sit and listen to the men and women of God pour their hearts and souls out to the congregation and tears fell from my eyes with every word. The Bible tells you that a broken heart and contrite spirit He will in no wise turn away, and not only my heart but my whole self was broken. I didn't see how, with all the wrong that I had done, this God was going to put me back together again.

There were a few times over that first three months in church when I would be so uncomfortable sitting there that I would have to run out of the church. But almost each time, one sister would come out to the parking lot and convince me to come back in the building.

I was broken and beaten, and only twenty-five years old. I was ready for God to change me completely, from the inside to the out. I went to my pastor and told him, "I'm ready to go down in Jesus' name, I want to be baptized."

The next Sunday, the elders prepared the baptismal pool while the mother of the church was in the back talking to me about what it meant to take on His name. I don't know if I really understood or heard all she was saying. I was asked to give a testimony of why I wanted to be baptized, and that testimony was very much like what you've read here so far. I felt so much better after my "confession." I knew that, as dirty and used up as I was, only God could wash my sins away.

The only people present at my baptism were the people from church and the woman who'd led me to it. My old life and lifestyle that I'd once lived was gone. The friends from those drug-house days had slowly left my life. I was drawn to the true light that healed my body, mind, and soul. My parents were still back in Maine and not churchgoers; they didn't need to be there with me. My daughter was with me, of course, and the pastor who sent that word directly from God himself was the man who baptized me. Singing "When the Saints Go Marching In," I was led to the water, and as I entered the pool, my mind was on the power of God and what He was going to do for me. The water was so cold and yet felt so good. I felt like my feet were being cleansed and eventually I was standing waist deep in the pool. My pastor said the words, "And now, my dear sister Deborah, I indeed baptize you in the name of Jesus Christ for the remission of your sins." And he leaned me back in the water, and when I came up I could hear the church singing "Washed in the Blood." I left my sins in that watery grave that same day.

God indeed cleaned my body and soul. When I came out of that water and put my church clothes on, I could smell the stench of cigarette smoke and it made me sick to my stomach. The smell of smoke permeated every article of clothing I had, even the clothes back in my closet, and I could no longer stand that smell. A woman from church blessed me with so many clothes that I never had to worry about putting those smoke-stained, smoke-soaked clothes back on again.

From that perfect day back in 1996 on, I never touched another cigarette or drug. The taste and the desire that I had for those things had left me with only the memories that I've shared with you in my writing. I can look back over those days at where I have come from and thank God that He made me a new person. For I have truly been changed.

Chapter Five

I remember jumping off the trestle in that small town in Maine and having only a few close friends that would often come to hang out on the boat on those warm summer days in the late eighties. That trestle was nestled above the lake with a short drop, maybe two stories until you hit the water. My friends and I would pull my parents' boat over to the bank there and tie it securely to a tree while we went up the hill to the trestle and waited for the first brave soul to jump, often encouraging that person to do it or they were a chicken.

I'll never forget the feeling of jumping. Not knowing if I'd break my neck in the shallow water below or if the wind would blow me into a rock that was very close. It was almost something you had to be precise about when you jumped, but as children, believing we were invincible, we just jumped without knowing how dangerous it was to jump into only four feet of water. Nobody really knew the trouble we put ourselves in every summer day in that secret spot, nor did they know how much fun it was to pack a picnic for the boat and spend entire summer days out on the lake, finding new adventures, new jumping places, and new waters within that lake to dive into off the boat.

Reflecting on my teenage years, at times I feel now, in my forties, that we do our children a disservice by telling them "You can be whatever you want to be when you grow up." It's easy to tell a child they can be whatever they want to be when they grow up, but we as parents need to be consciously informing our children of the realities of life when you choose the wrong path, the wrong friends. Let them know that what you do in your young-adult life or late teenage years can affect you in the future.

I am transparent with my children. I want them to know that the bad choices I made led me down many wrong paths in life. Being authentic with my children has kept them with good grades and led them to be examples within our community, leaving me proud that I am able to share my mistakes with them in hopes that they don't repeat what I went through.

Being adopted at five months old, I never experienced a hard life growing up. My mother was at the time married to a psychiatrist; in fact, Dr. Green was the head of Lighthouse Hospital's psychiatry department. However, he had a secret that thankfully I don't remember too much. He was an alcoholic, and he and my mother divorced when I was around three or four. I can only recall him dropping me off on Davis Avenue at the house and leaving, and never seeing him again until I was a confused and hurt seventeen-year-old. My mother remarried when I was seven and my dad adopted me, officially making me his daughter, Deborah Schrepper!

Tears fall from my eyes when I think of how unselfish my father was and how he loved my mother enough to include me in the whole package, not knowing that his daughter would be more than a challenge as she grew up and, at times, even in adulthood. I wonder, if he could go back in time, would he think twice? Am I a disappointment to him? To my mother? To my three children, or even to myself? Those are the questions that fill my own thoughts when I reflect on my life and the choices I've made in past moments, and I often find myself daydreaming about turning back the hands of time-- how far would I have to go back? Twenty years, maybe twenty-five, or push it and just turn it back forty-one years? Impulsive, active, friendly, compassionate... disorganized, cluttered: adjectives that I could use to describe myself at times.

Chapter Six

Nobody told me at nineteen that I "didn't know everything," or even that I "didn't know anything yet." Well, in retrospect, my parents, teachers, and older family members did indeed tell me, and often; I suppose I was too self-centered to listen, or perhaps wanted to experience my very own journey. Seriously, when we're at that age we can't wait to become adults, grownups, mature individuals, right?

When a pipe leaked or the sump pump stopped working, my parents would call a plumber. When my dad needed to have, wiring put in the basement, he hired an electrician. As an adolescent, I watched my parents call on repair people when my dad was unsure how to fix something or wanted something remodeled. So, I know now, as an adult, whom to call when tangible things are broken. But a question I didn't know the answer to when I was young was, whom do we call when we find that it is our self that is broken and in need of spiritual, emotional, transformational fixing? It took walking through the fires of my life to believe that I was beautiful despite my growing in the mud, that I possessed the beauty by having my own lotus-flower journey.

About the Author

Deborah Elizabeth Schrepper, born in 1971, is the
Founder and CEO of Harvesting Life's Lessons.
She was born to a heroin addict and placed up for
adoption. Her birth mother's boyfriend and pimp
told her, "We aren't keeping any mixed babies." In
Her Secret Sins, Deborah addresses some personal
life lessons she's learned along her journey as a
single mother, a nurse, and a three-time published
author of a book series, *Harvesting Life's Lessons*,
followed now by *Her Secret Sins*. She is a requested
National Speaker and a certified Holistic Personal
Development Coach, using a myriad of personal
stories about overcoming many challenges to engage
all walks of life. As a Holistic Personal Development
Coach, she continues to grow in knowledge and
encourage others to learn to overcome the organized
chaos that surrounds each of us. She began
Harvesting Life's Lessons with a clear purpose and
vision: to L.I.V.E. (Lend Individuals a Variety of
Encouragement). She is a woman of strong faith,

and she gives back to her community in a variety of ways, including serving as a board member on two local nonprofit organizations. She is diligent and determined to spread the message of H.O.P.E. (Help Others Persevere and Endure) to those who have walked, and perhaps remain walking, through similar challenges as she once did herself. Having overcome those rough terrains, which can still cause a tear to fall from her eyes, she uses those obstacles as tools to climb to higher plateaus, harvesting the lessons of experiences from a painful, messy past. Her mission and vision is simple: to inspire you to keep climbing your mountains, knowing that you are not alone. There is always HOPE! Keep climbing through good and bad, which you will overcome, and eventually you will bravely share your life lessons with others. Life is a gift, new every day, that we unwrap with excitement, embracing its contents. Every new day that appears teaches us to walk in our purpose and brings us one step closer to the top of the mountain!